Feeling Small
Walking Tall

Feeling Small Walking Tall

MARIE CHAPIAN

BETHANY HOUSE PUBLISHERS
MINNEAPOLIS, MINNESOTA 55438
A Division of Bethany Fellowship, Inc.

Photos by Dick Easterday.

We wish to thank the young people of Action for Teens youth group, Bethany Missionary Church, Bloomington, Minnesota, whose photos appear on the pages of this book.

Published by Bethany House Publishers
A Division of Bethany Fellowship, Inc.
6820 Auto Club Road, Minneapolis, Minnesota 55438

Printed in the United States of America

Library of Congress Cataloging-in-Publication Data

Chapian, Marie.
    Feeling small walking tall / Marie Chapian.
       p. cm.
    Summary: A collection of daily devotions and Bible verses for teen-agers, discussing such topics as interpersonal relations, school, and family life.
      1. Teenagers—Prayer-books and devotions—English.
[1. Prayer books and devotions.]   I. Title.
BV4850.C49   1989
242'.63—dc20   89–36271
ISBN 1-55661-029-7   CIP

To Christa and Liza

MARIE CHAPIAN, Ph.D., is known around the world as an author and speaker. She also is a Christian counselor and a familiar personality to radio and TV audiences. She has written twenty-four books with translations in eleven languages.

Contents

7

Dream Catcher

I want to be a dream catcher—
    a person who can walk through trials
        without cringing in fear
    or lashing out in anger
        when things don't go quite right.

I want to be a dream catcher
    of dreams that are my own.
        Free to dream them
    and to change them because
        the Lord knows
    I'm growing and changing every day.

I want to be a dream catcher—
    a person who won't stumble
        when pride sticks out its foot.
    I want to walk steadily on,
        my face set toward the cross of Christ.

I want to be a dream catcher,
    discovering the thoughts of God
        and His love in every corner,
    reflecting the reality of that love
        to people, old and young.

———

I want to be a dream catcher.
    And though I'm jealous at times
        when I see my dreams caught
by someone else, the Dream Maker
        reminds me:
Heaven will never run out of dreams.

Introduction

I am praying that I have captured on the following pages even some of the energy, vitality, sensitivity and intelligence I have discovered in the young people I know as students and friends. Young people just like you. I have put their words to free verse, and allowed their voices to speak for themselves. Through the interplay of thoughts, dreams and the prayers of teens and adults alike; they represent the people who live in your world . . . mine too.

My work as a Christian counselor and teacher gives me the great privilege of knowing and working with many young people. As an author, I receive letters from teenagers who share their hopes and dreams and this book is the result of my dialogue with them.

Perhaps you will recognize yourself here. My hope is that you will see yourself through God's eyes and discover every single day what God already knows about you: that you are valuable to this world. Your feelings, thoughts, dreams and ideas are important to Him because they're yours and *you* are important to Him.

I suggest that you read one devotion a day and think about that truth during the day. You could probably read the entire book in one sitting, but you'll get more out of it if you read in small doses. I've added my own little note as a Thought for the Day at the end of each chapter, and a scripture verse to memorize and think about. I pray you'll be encouraged to be a dream catcher.

There will be many voices speaking in this book. I hope you recognize one above all the others, that of the Savior who calls out, "You're mine. *I positively love you.*"

Marie Chapian

Part One

FEELING SMALL

Chapter 1

Are You Listening, God?

Felicia:

Heather and Mike have been going together
for a whole year now.
Everybody knows they are a couple.
If you talk to Mike you say, "How's Heather?"
and when you talk to Heather
you always ask about Mike.
Everybody figures they'll get married
someday after we all graduate.
They're even planning to go to Bible college together.
I want a relationship like theirs.
Sometimes I get real jealous of Heather.
It makes me mad when she has
a terrific boyfriend
and I don't have
anybody.

––––––––––

I get depressed thinking
I'll probably never have a boyfriend like Mike,
who is so sweet and such a good Christian.

I try to trust the Lord,
to have faith and all,
but it doesn't help.
God might just pass me by
and give all the good boyfriends
to all the other girls.
I could wind up an old maid.
I'll become an old lady missionary
in some forsaken tropical village,
wearing clunky shoes and an awful hairdo,
with my letters from home growing moss on the shelf.
(I admitted this to my mother.
She just laughed at me and said
at least then I wouldn't have to worry
about my weight.
I don't think that's funny.)
At our high school church retreat

we had this speaker who told us if we focus on others,
God will answer our prayers
when we're not looking.

———————

Dear Lord, I am not looking.

Thought for Today:

Does God really and truly care enough to answer your prayers? Will God answer Felicia's prayer for a boyfriend? How about your prayers for a boyfriend (or a girlfriend)? Do you think God answers only when you're not looking?

P.S. Is there a Mike or a Heather in your life whom you're jealous of, too?

W ait for the Lord;
Be strong, and let your heart take
     courage;
Yes, wait for the Lord. (Psalm 27:14)

Chapter 2

Where Am I Going?

Bob:

You wake up in the middle of the night
   and walk barefoot to the kitchen,
   open the refrigerator.
It's not food you want,
   but you slump into a chair
and reach for the bag of chocolate chip cookies.
   Munching away, you feel hollow inside,
like you're a song nobody knows the words to;
it's hopeless, it will always be this way you think.
There you are, in a sleeping house
   while the world outside
is spinning with life and action.
Right now someone your age in Tokyo is writing essays,
   taking an exam, having lunch, walking arm in arm,
but you are
stuck in zerosville,
   between asleep and awake,
   hot and cold,
   real and fake.

———

Lately you've begun to wonder
    what you're going to do with your life.
Your friends are talking about *being* this and that,
    and you wonder if you really know these people at all.
When did they start thinking so old?
    Kerry, a *doctor*?
    Jim, an *architect*?
    Jeremy, a *minister*?
    What will you be?
You crumple the empty cookie bag
    and pad across the cold tile to the freezer
    where the peppermint ice cream
        lurks behind the string beans.
You stand eating ice cream out of the carton
and wonder what kind of future you'd have as a rock star
    or a politician maybe.
A paper boy.
A stock broker.
Why is everyone in such a hurry to *be* something?
What's wrong with the way things are?
    You'd be satisfied with a girlfriend
        and a few good marks on your report card.
Pulling yourself up on the kitchen counter
    and curling your feet beneath you,
you squint out the window over the sink
at the shadowy moon outside.
At what point in Jeremy's life
did he say to himself,
       "I am going to be a minister"?
    When exactly in Kerry's life
       did she know without a doubt her destiny was
medicine?
Your mother tells you not to worry,
    God will lead you,
but *where*?
       That's the question.
    Don't you hate it?

Everybody seems to be going someplace,
   and you're half dressed in the kitchen,
      stuffed on cookies and ice cream.
It's 3 a.m., but you're wide awake,
   and you can do nothing but wait.
Wait for sleep or morning, whichever comes first.
You shuffle across the floor to your room
   high on sugar
      and still hungry.

Thought for Today

Your life is not a minor detail to God. He doesn't try to shake you off so He can get His work done without distractions. He won't lead you to some corner and say "Wait here until I get back" and then desert you.

The way to recognize the leading of God is to KNOW GOD. Put away your ice cream. Close up the cookie bag. Listen: " 'I know the plans that I have for you,' declares the Lord. 'Plans for welfare and not for calamity to give you a future and a hope' " (Jeremiah 29:11). Understand that, and you may not have such problems sleeping.

Commit your way to the Lord, trust also in Him, and He will do it. (Psalm 37:5)

Chapter 3

Is Anybody Thinking About Me?

Dawn:

I think that nobody in the whole world
is thinking about me right now.
I think that I am the only one
who is thinking about me.
That must mean when I go to sleep
and my thoughts stand still,
I no longer exist to anyone—
not even to me.
Sometimes when I am walking
or riding my bike
or doing some everyday thing,
I imagine someone loves me
and is watching me at that very moment.
My great-aunt who died last summer
really loved me and even spoiled me.
Sometimes I wish that she could still watch me
like an invisible camera
or a mom from a kitchen window,
proud and smiling.
But then I remember

I'm not a little kid anymore,
and people think of you differently
when you're older.
They stop talking to you and start asking questions.
"What are you going to do
when you finish school?"
"Are you going to college? What college?"
"Got a boyfriend?" "Got a girlfriend?"
I answer their questions and they're satisfied,
but I'm not.
Maybe it's too much to expect
to be in someone's thoughts.
And maybe I wouldn't even
be happy there.

Thought for Today:

The psalmist says, "How precious to me are your thoughts, O God! How vast is the sum of them! Were I to count them, they would outnumber the grains of sand. When I awake, I am still with you" (Psalm 139:17, NIV).

There are times when nobody is directing loving thoughts toward us. Sometimes people don't put our best interests first. Even kind, loving people are capable of thinking more about themselves than they do about you.

To a small child it's normal to believe the entire world revolves around him or her. There is no other world to a child than the one he or she knows. No other concerns, needs, wants or thoughts are as real as their own. As you grow and develop, you become increasingly aware of a world outside your own, until as a young adult you have finally developed a sense of the world around you and your place in it.

Still, it's not easy to be anonymous.

Who thinks about you? I'll tell you who.

God thinks about you far more than any mortal could imagine. He thinks eternal, mighty, glorious thoughts toward you, the kind that surpass interruption and limitations of human speech. You are always in His thoughts.

Search me, O God, and know my heart;
Try me and know my anxious thoughts;
And see if there be any hurtful way in me,
And lead me in the everlasting way.
(Psalm 139:23–24)

Chapter 4

Lord, Keep Me From Falling

Becky:

Every day there are a zillion temptations, Lord.
    It's *raining* sin out there,
and every time I step outside
    I get pelted in the face
with dark invitations and
    forbidden delights.
"Just say no," they insist.
    I try.
I turn away
    but sometimes I feel deprived.
I get to thinking
    when I'm home alone,
and I wonder if
    I'm missing all the fun.
Can I be happy here
where God keeps blessing me?
    And will I be wise enough
to stay here?

Thought for Today:

It's healthy to talk about temptations. Admitting our temptations is the first step to overcoming them. Everyone is tempted by something; and our frailty is our very ticket to strength. Of course you're tempted! Of course sin looks good. Sometimes it looks like the non-Christians are having all the fun, but your resolve to love God and live a clean, pure life is not up to you alone. You have the Holy Spirit within you to empower and encourage you.

Teenagers often find that it's difficult to be in worldly situations and maintain a Christian lifestyle—especially in public high school. And I'll tell you something: it's going to be difficult when you get out of high school, too. The world is everywhere—on the bus, in the office, at the beach, in the theater, museums, sidewalks, train stations, airports, newspapers, books. And here we are in the middle of it all. But I see you as a light on a hill, shining magnificently in spite of yourself. Don't despair at temptation. You'll make it. You'll come out on top. No matter how sorely you're tempted, the Holy Spirit is always there to pull you out of sin's grip. Hang in there, especially with your Christian friends and leaders. Talk about your feelings. Pray with them. You'll see that Jesus is the Lord of Lords who enables you to overcome. He's your Lord and will not let you fall.

No temptation has overtaken you but such as is common to man; and God is faithful, who will not allow you to be tempted beyond what you are able, but with the temptation will provide the way of escape also, that you may be able to endure it. (1 Corinthians 10:13)

Chapter 5

I Know You, but Who Am I?

Mark:

One of the jocks called me a wimp;
   and the worst thing about it is,
   I think it's true.
I compete with the guys,
   always joking around,
   acting tough, looking macho,
big bad me.
I don't like myself
   or them
   very much at all.
I sometimes wonder who I am,
   what I'm really like.
It's easy to know
   what everybody else likes,
and it's easy to be
   what everybody expects,
but maybe I'm not really what they think.
   How can I be sure when
I don't even know
   what I think?

When I was little, my mother told her sisters
that God gave her a son like me
as a trial of her faith,
to endure the fellowship of suffering.
Now she shakes her head
    and rolls her eyes to the ceiling.
Depending on how loud I am,
    or what I've just tipped over or stumbled into,
    or how many loaves of bread or gallons of milk
        I've consumed, she will talk about
    overcoming and being granted
    to sit down with the Lord
        on His throne.
I don't ever remember her holding me
    or telling me I was a good boy.

When I graduate from high school,
    I *have* to go to college.
My parents decided that.
Sometimes I see myself as a sports star,
but I think I could also be a medical doctor
to the Ogala
or a Bible translator to the Zapotec of Oaxaca.
My dad says
computer science is the field of promise,
so I may just wind up computer programming
behind a desk.

So first I have to go to college.
That means I get four more years
of goofing off, trying to be a jock.
But hey, the women are lined up. . . .
Why am I getting all disjointed?
    I have all the time in the world
        to decide who I am . . . but tell me:
Why do you think
    my mother never held me?

Thought for Today

These words, spoken to me in total honesty, were hard to hear. Mark believed, from his earliest recollection, that he was a bad person. He learned to see himself as a puppet, someone *playing* at being someone. The truth is, he was a well-liked guy, athletic, popular with girls, and a lot of fun. Everyone around him thought he was a happy-go-lucky, carefree person. But deep inside he was not happy. He was still looking for himself.

Inside he felt his mother knew the *real* person he was and that person was an awful one. Everybody else, he believed, saw only an outer, superficial shell. So no matter how good or macho or accomplished he might be, underneath it all he still felt unhuggable, irrepressible, a burden, a "trial of the faith."

It's important to understand who you *are*, what you are *made of* and what you are *worth.* If you don't, you, too, can go through high school and college in a sort of fog, not knowing where you're going or why.

Jesus not only gives us purpose, He gives us value and worth. He says the kingdom of God belongs to His children (Luke 18:16). The Lord has had His hand on you; He has a great purpose for your life.

Ask yourself whose opinion you value most. Whose idea of who you are do you agree with?

Do you believe you are loved enough, valuable enough to die for? Jesus did.

> And you are in Him, made full and have come to fullness of life—in Christ you too are filled with the Godhead: Father, Son and Holy Spirit, and reach full spiritual stature. And He is the Head of all rule and authority—of every angelic principality and power. (Colossians 2:10, Amp.)

Chapter 6

Your Picture

Prayer is like a camera
    that takes pictures of the heart
for God.
    He, in turn,
examines, ponders,
    concludes.
Give Him the portraits
    and the candids, the still lifes, and the action shots.
Show Him your work
    before you frame it.
"Ah, yes," says God, "I know this one well."
    With arms open, He receives every prayer.
Even indistinct scribbles,
    like marks made with a stick in sand.
No picture made for God goes unnoticed,
    rejected or cast aside.
And when the angels see you coming every day,
    hauling your prayers on shoulders made strong
with carrying your pictures to Him,
    they say to one another,

"How familiar to us is the Lord's Beloved."
They, too, know you by your picture.
The picture that reminds them of Jesus.

Thought for Today:

Your prayers are beautiful and powerful. Write them down, give them to God every day. Talk to Him always. He listens. He loves you, and by this friendship with Him you become more and more like Him.

And we, who with unveiled faces all reflect the Lord's glory, are being transformed into his likeness with ever-increasing glory, which comes from the Lord, who is the Spirit. (2 Corinthians 3:18, NIV)

Part Two

GETTING THERE

Chapter 7

Nobody Really Noticed

Paul:

Ronny sat alone in the back of the room mostly.
He never raised his hand
or seemed to be all that interested in anything.
He would stare out the window
or read history when he was supposed to be doing math.
Nobody really paid much attention to him.
Sometimes he would talk to himself, and at lunch
you'd see him walking alone
around the football field,
his hands moving as though
he were rehearsing an argument.
He rode his bike to school,
and almost nobody in our class rode bikes.
His face was shadowy and bluish,
and when you got near him
he jumped back, frightened.
We never thought about that.
Once in p.e. he caught the ball
and instead of throwing it back,
he just kept going with it.

His long spidery legs pranced away and
nobody yelled at him to bring the ball back.
Later in class he had a tiny smile on his face.
He grew thinner and bluer, now that I think back,
but nobody really noticed.
He was just Ronny-at-the-back-of-the-room.
Then on a Tuesday morning last spring
when everything outside was getting green
our homeroom teacher told us gravely
Ronny would not be back to school.
He was dead. His father,
who had broken more than twenty
of Ronny's bones in the past,
had killed him this time.
For a week the teachers talked about
"child abuse," "murder," "tragedy."
All the words that described Ronny
who sat in the back of the room
where nobody really noticed.

Thought for Today:

Everybody needs a friend. Maybe somebody near you, someone you've never thought of before, could use your friendship right now. Will you ask the Lord to give you a concern for others and to touch somebody's life through you today? Remember Ronny. His story may have been different if he'd had a friend; if somebody had noticed.

Since I am afflicted and needy,
Let the Lord be mindful of me;
Thou art my help and my deliverer;
Do not delay, O my God. (Psalm 40:17)

Chapter 8

Different

Becky:

Being different can be a dangerous thing.
You never know when you'll find yourself
alone . . . in the dark . . . on the outer edge
with nobody who understands you
or wants to be your friend.
That's scary.
So why try anything new?
Why try to think new thoughts
or dream big
or aim high?
I wonder—did God create us
all to be alike?
To look alike, act alike
and have the same ideas and thoughts?
I wonder—do I have to dress like you
and do my hair like you
and worry about being what you want me to be?
I don't want to be *too* different.
but more than that, I don't want to be
you.

Thought for Today:

Individuality is a precious gift from God that challenges us to be creative, to explore our world and to reach our full potential in Christ.

Sometimes that is hard. Nobody wants to be *too* different. But being different can cause trouble when you go to extremes breaking the "social code." You can alienate others with ultra-radical looks and behavior. Adults call it rebellion.

Instead, why not revolt against mindless conformity and exclusiveness? You won't get anywhere by hiding in a smug little mold that is only big enough for a few.

Nothing big and beautiful can emerge from a place where there's little individuality. Throw away the prejudices and biases that prevent you from enjoying your own creative personality and those of the others around you.

May you really come to know—practically, through experience for yourself—the love of Christ, which far surpasses mere knowledge (without experience); that you may be filled (through all your being) unto all the fullness of God—[that is] may have the richest measure of the divine Presence, and become a body wholly filled and flooded with God Himself! (Ephesians 3:19, Amp.)

Chapter 9

The New Girl

Felicia:

In speech class each of us
had to give a five-minute talk about ourselves.
I wondered if I had anything
interesting to say
and if everybody would laugh at me
when I finished.
On the day we began our speeches,
this new girl I didn't know got up.
Real quiet, she says,
"My mom has been married four times
and my dad's been married five times.
I guess you might say
I come from a dysfunctional family.
It's hard on a kid when you don't know
where you'll sleep at night."
Then she talked about moving around, being unwanted,
and how happy she was
to finally be at our school
and living *on her own.*
That got me: *On her own.*

She was sixteen, I figured,
like the rest of us.
I tried to imagine
this skinny, plain girl
on her own,
frying her own hamburgers,
washing her own towels and paying *bills.*
She left quickly after class that day.
The next week I had to give my speech—
about our family's summer vacation to Washington, D.C.
(where I *boiled* in the heat).
I looked at the new girl across the room.
Her stringy hair hung over her ears,
her pouty little mouth was chewing the end of a pencil,
and those huge, pale eyes
filled with a strange look I'd never seen before.

———————

One day I was late to speech class, and I bumped into her
in the hall outside the classroom door.
"I liked your speech,"
she said.
"I've always wanted to go to Washington."
She looked at me intently
with her large green eyes.
For a second I thought we would be friends,
and I could bring her around
to all the "in" happenings
and get her in the "in" group.
Then maybe she'd try out for cheerleading
and go out with the "in" guys,
and I would invite her to my party on Friday night.
Then she said, "But I feel sorry for you.
It must be really rough
having all your decisions made for you."
I never told a soul what she said,
but it really ticked me off.

She thought I was a *shallow* person.

————

Later we had to give our second speech,
on some important issue.
We all wondered what
we should talk about.
I figured cleaning up the beaches was good,
and my girl friend Barbara decided to talk
on the importance of wardrobe color coordination.
(She'd already done the research.)
Then the new girl,
whose name I still didn't know,
gets up.
This time her hair is clean and shiny,
and I think to myself she's cute
in a skinny out-of-touch sort of way.
"The issue is *survival*," she informs us,
and then she gives this speech that was so powerful
it would have brought tears to the eyes
of Socrates.

————

I'm so depressed.

Thought for Today:

Have you ever questioned your own values? Felicia
thought she was better than the new girl. But was she? Do
you think you are better than some people because you
are more popular, or smarter, or better looking than they
are? One way to evaluate what's important is to see yourself as Jesus does. Your speeches may not impress Socrates, but do they reach God? If you were to give a speech
about the most important thing in your life, what would
that be?

But God has chosen the foolish things of the world to shame the wise, and God has chosen the weak things of the world to shame the things which are strong, and the base things of the world and the despised, God has chosen, the things that are not, that He might nullify the things that are.
(1 Corinthians 1:27–28)

Chapter 10

Limiting
Yourself

"So you made a mistake. Big deal!"
      said Arnold's live-in grandma.
"So what? Do you really think
      that anyone is talking about you or your problems?"
Yes, thought Arnold. *The whole school.*
      At this very instant.
Arnold's grandmother was unimpressed
      with his silence.
In just a few years' time, she said,
      no one on the face of the earth would give
two hoots
      about Arnold's Big Mistake.
"What's one *faux pas,* more or less?
      You'll make a million mistakes in your lifetime.
Can't let each one get you down like this,
      or you'll never get to be an old person."
But Arnold wasn't listening.
      There is only one way out of this mess, he figured.
He'd go back to school and lie.
      Maybe if he was convincing enough,

they would believe him.
Lying is better than running away anyhow.
He'd tell the coach:
  "The reason I fell on my rear end
    at such a crucial moment in the soccer game
    is because I was having an attack.
  I have this rare eye disease
  where fast-moving objects
    appear invisible at certain times of the day. . . ."
No good.
Then he'd have to quit soccer.
That night, the phone didn't ring. Not once.
  Not even his best friend, Kevin, called.
Arnold decided he was all alone in the world,
  forsaken and disgraced.

Thought for Today:

How is Arnold limiting himself? Why doesn't his grandmother's advice make him feel better?

It is OK to make a mistake. Really. It may not be pleasant or comfortable, but it's OK. If you are horrified at the thought of doing something dumb or falling on your rear end at a crucial moment, you'll never try anything new and you'll never venture out to do anything heroic or wonderful. As a child of God you can be courageous and daring. Christians are people with strong convictions and integrity, but they are not perfect. Sometimes they make mistakes. Then they go on.

How would you end Arnold's story?

I press on toward the goal for the prize of the upward call of God in Christ Jesus. (Philippians 3:14)

Chapter 11

The Illusionist

Bob:

A magician on TV today
had his assistant
shoot at a balloon with a dart gun.
What made the trick cool was this:
The magician held the balloon
in front of his face.
As the drums rolled, the gun went off
and the balloon popped.
The magician staggered and then threw his hands up
triumphantly
and spit a dart out of his mouth.
(I thought it was boring.)
Those tricks—sawing ladies in half,
pulling white birds from behind scarves,
asking you to pick a number that is "miraculously"
the same number written on a slip of paper
inside the cuff of the magician's jacket—
they're all so gimmicky.
So much manipulation.
Just like I am when I pretend to be

what I'm not.
I think some of the greatest illusionists
are not professional magicians at all,
but the people who
manipulate others
every day
to get what they want.

Thought for Today:

Selfishness is being so involved with ourselves and our own world that we maneuver everything around us to our best advantage. It's important to dump the "magician" way of thinking. Selfishness is sin. The illusionist deceives as does the manipulator. Both want you to believe in what isn't real. There is a difference, though. One uses slight-of-hand for the purpose of entertainment and the other deceives for self-serving, personal gain. Have you ever pretended to be very friendly with someone you hardly know or care about because you wanted to borrow his class notes? Do you or her kiss up to a teacher so you'll be noticed—and ultimately receive a better grade? Think of some of your own pretenses. Then answer this: Why is being real important?

*F*or the Lord gives wisdom;
From His mouth come knowledge and
   understanding.
He stores up sound wisdom for the
   upright;
He is a shield to those who walk in
   integrity. (Proverbs 2:6–7)

Chapter 12

Reexamining "Right"

Two artists began to paint.
One was an impatient girl
who wanted a picture immediately
and didn't want to spend much time on it.
The other knew the value of care
and precision in her work.
So she didn't rush.
Both knew that a canvas must be primed
with a special medium before paint is applied.
But the first artist said,
"I don't want to prime my canvas.
It takes too long."
The second artist took care
to prime hers carefully.
She waited for it to dry before applying paint.
The first artist finished her picture
way ahead of the second artist,
who took many weeks
before she was able to say, "Done."
The first artist's painting

was blotched with patchy color,
and before long the painting cracked
and the canvas sagged.
But the second artist's picture
was shiny and evenly stretched,
its images carefully drawn.
How do you suppose the first artist felt
about her hasty work?
Was she delighted?
Did she exclaim, "I like the effect I've created.
It's new and different, and I can learn from it"?
If you think that's what she said,
you are right.

Thought for Today:

It's true that careful, methodical work usually brings the best results. But if we think it's the *only* way to do something, we might be limiting ourselves, boxing ourselves into a corner.

Some art is wonderful because it's spontaneous, and some art is wonderful because it has been painstakingly created over a long period of time. The same is true of music. Are the simple Christian choruses we sing in church any less meaningful than, say, a piece by Beethoven or Handel? Aren't both types of music used to glorify God?

Teenagers tend to put heavy pressure on themselves to achieve great things; sometimes the concept of "great" needs to be examined. Can you allow yourself to paint a painting somebody else might think is bad? Would you allow somebody *else* to paint a picture you don't like without judging them?

How about some other area of your life? Sports . . . schoolwork . . . Is it really crucial that you always be *right*?

*I*t was for freedom that Christ set us free . . . (Galatians 5:1a)

Chapter 13

Being a Giver

Jim:

Even though I'm
   probably younger than you,
I want to share an important discovery
   I've learned
   about catching dreams.
I never thought I could be of any real help
to anybody, or important and needed by anybody—
   especially to healthy, well-adjusted *adults.*
But my dream is to serve God, to help someone.
   And what do you know? I've done just that.
I learned that it's not only hurting people
   we can help.
   Not only the lost souls
on the highway of life,
   but the *found* ones
leading comfortable lives
as well.
Everybody can use a blessing.

Thought for Today:

Some people think that the only way to serve the Lord is to be a missionary overseas. Others think the only way to serve the Lord is to go to seminary and become an ordained minister. The fact is, we serve the Lord every day of our lives. You are His servant as you go to school, or to band practice, football and baseball games. You serve Him wherever you are—at your job, at home, or at church. When you are nice to the mailman, the Lord touches that person through you because the Holy Spirit dwells in you. If you are honest, fair, kind and just, you are expressing the attributes of God. It's important to remember that you have a special gift—the ability to bless everyone in your life in some way of your own. Take a few minutes right now to pray that the Lord will guide and direct you as you seek to do good in His name. You need the power of the Holy Spirit to do this; you cannot do it on your own.

For you were called to freedom, brethren; only do not turn your freedom into an opportunity for the flesh, but through love serve one another. (Galatians 5:13)

Chapter 14

Every Time

Nancy:

Every time I try to do something neat,
　　something *else* comes along
　　　　to mess it up.
　　I'm sick of trying.
Why do I keep thinking
　　I can do something right
　　　　when I never do?
Nobody even helps me
　　or really cares;
　　　　and even if they did,
　　it wouldn't matter
because I don't think I matter.

Arnold:

Guys aren't supposed to cry.
　　That makes me feel like a wimp
because lots of times
　　I wish I could cry.

Instead, I'm expected
    to fight back,
        even when I don't want to,
    take pain *like a man*.
        Whatever that means.
My dad swears and throws things
    when he's upset.
Personally, I don't think
    that's acting like a man.

————

At school I never let on
    I'm a virgin.
The guys would crucify me.
    "Nobody's supposed to be
        a virgin at eighteen."
    And nobody, ever, should
        admit it if he is.
Living up to my Christian values
    is tough when there aren't
        many Christians in my school.
    At times it's lonely being weird.
I sent in my application
    to a Christian college.
        I just pray I make it.

Jill:

I may not do everything right,
    but do I *have* to freak out
        every time I fail?
    I'd spend a lot of time
        just freaking out.
You know, nobody ever pats me on the back
    for being "a good girl."
For my seventeenth birthday,

my mother gave me a bottle
of birth control pills
and some condoms.
"Better safe than sorry," she said.
Talk about no communication.
They must think that all this time
I spend in church
serving as president of the youth group
is just a joke.

––––––––––

Either God is real, or He isn't.
Either you love Him, or you don't.
I do. And I'm going on with Jesus.
You can choose to feel sorry for yourself,
or you can choose happiness and peace.
I've chosen happiness.
I hope you do, too.

Thought for Today:

God puts His answers within you by His Spirit. He is building wisdom in you. He wants to make your spirit responsive to His leading. How wonderful when you let Him do just that, even when the world pushes you to go its way instead of His way.

I delight to do Your will, O my God;
yes, Your law is within my heart.
(Psalm 40:8, Amp.)

Chapter 15

Feeling Guilty for Feeling Good?

Dawn

Last year, there was this girl Twyla in our school. She was nice and all that, but man . . . she was SO FAT! When we were picked up from school, she took up practically the whole back seat of a car.

She was touchy about it, too. If anybody talked about things like clothes or summer (which meant the beach, which meant swim suits), she'd clam right up. We knew she was mad at us for talking about things that embarrassed her.

"You're just making fun of me," she'd say.

Once she got mad because Barbara and I were talking about our aerobics class. Barbara said she thought she had actual *cellulite* on her thighs. We just never knew what would tick Twyla off. She said we were just showing off.

One day when we were coming from chorus I said I would never in my entire life eat chocolate ice cream again because I hated the color. Twyla stopped dead in her tracks, like something had stung her.

She surprised me. "Me too," she exclaimed.

So Twyla and I hated chocolate ice cream together. It

was sort of a fraternal secret we shared. And from that day on, I could mention bicycle riding, size three clothes, and even swim suits without Twyla frowning miserably.

Still, we all felt guilty when we were around Twyla. We could run without gasping and sweating, even going up and down stairs. We didn't get tired as easily as she did. And we all had boyfriends, except her.

It made us feel bad because, for some reason, Twyla made us feel as if it was OUR fault she was not normal like us. Like God had given her a Fat Handicap. It made us look at our own handicaps, sometimes, and ask ourselves whom we blamed for them.

To this day I can't eat chocolate ice cream.

Thought for Today

When we say "It's not my fault," what are we REALLY saying?

> Never pay back evil for evil to any-one. Respect what is right in the sight of all people. If possible, so far as it depends on you, be at peace with all men. (Romans 12:17–18)

Chapter 16

Names That Stick

There was this guy they called Bad Bart
(really—can you believe it?)
    who lived in a real small town.
His family belonged
    to a real small church.
Bad Bart went to a small school too.
    A private, Christian school.
He didn't do too well;
    he was always last in his class.
The kids made fun of him.
So did his dad and his brother.
    They called him Dumb Bart,
and pretty soon he believed he was dumb.
    He went to youth group and
he liked a girl named Heather.
    Cute girl, smart and kind.
But Heather didn't like Bart one bit
    because he always acted so dumb.
That made Bart sad
    and mad.

Pretty soon everything was making Bart sad and
    mostly mad.
One day he got into a fight
    with his brother and another guy,
        and his mother called him a bad seed,
        rotten to the core.
        The teacher put him down
        and so did the kids in school.
Pretty soon he believed he was bad,
    and the name Bad Bart just stuck.
A few years later after another fight,
    in a bar,
    he was wandering down a dirty back street
in a big city,
        carrying a half-empty bottle.
    He came upon a tatoo parlor.
There were pictures
of fish, snakes, beasts and monsters
    displayed on the wall inside.
He saw the one that said it best.
    "I'll take this one," said Bad Bart.
That was the day he had
    Born to Lose
tattooed on his back
    forever.

Thought for Today:

Being a Christian doesn't guarantee you'll be kind and understanding all the time. What names do you give people? Are they the same names Jesus knows them by? Do you believe the negative things others say about you? And how about the names you call yourself? What gives any of us the right to criticize a beautiful part of God's creation? Your name—who you *are*—is tattooed on the palm of God's hand. Believe it.

> *B*ehold, I have inscribed you on the palms of My hands; your walls are continually before Me. (Isaiah 49:16)

Chapter 17

A Way Out

Let the weak say, "I am strong . . ." (Joel 3:10b).

Do you think of yourself as a weak person?
   Have you ever felt utterly helpless?
Hopeless?
   Ever felt there was no way out
of your troubles
   and you'd always be doomed to
failure?
   God tells us that
when there is no further down
we can go,
the bottom will drop out on us
   and we will find beneath our feet
   the solid Rock.
   Jesus.

Thought for Today:

There's more to you than you often think there is. It may be that your problem isn't weakness at all, but your lack of vision. Ask God to *show* you what your strengths are, and how they can be used for Him!

Do you not know? Have you not
    heard?
The Everlasting God, the Lord,
The Creator of the ends of the earth
    does not become weary or tired . . .
He gives strength to the weary,
And to him who lacks might He
    increases power.
Though youths grow weary and tired,
And vigorous young men stumble
    badly,
Yet those who wait for the Lord
Will gain new strength;
They will mount up with wings like
    eagles,
They will run and not get tired,
They will walk and not become weary.
(Isaiah 40:28-31)

Chapter 18

Special

Shelly:

I was going to be a ballerina.
    I started ballet lessons when I was three.
We have pictures of me in my *tutu*,
    standing in fifth position,
hands in the air.
    I don't look at those pictures anymore.
It seems strange to think of the way I am now.
    They call me *special* now.
        In *special* classes,
        with other *special* people
        in wheelchairs.
After the accident, my friends were great.
    They came to the hospital every day,
        sent cards and candy, books and games.
    I have a million stuffed animals now.
But I can't walk with my friends or go upstairs.
    And at the movies
I have to sit in back.
    The driver who hit me was drunk.
Mom joined MADD.

They changed the whole house around
    to make room for my wheelchair.
Everything is *special* now.
Even our car.
    I'm amazed God let me live;
the doctor's didn't give much hope.
    I can hear and see,
        and hold things in my hands.
    I can feed myself and read
        and feel the rain.
    I can laugh and sing
        and because of tutors
    I'll graduate with my class.
And though my legs won't hold me up,
in the dark, when I'm alone,
    I think I'm still a ballerina.

Thought for Today:

Some call physically disabled people *handicapped.*
Others call them *special.* Handicapped people *are* special;
they often have an appreciation for life that many "normal" people don't have. Shelly is grateful to be able to see
and hear and smell and feel the rain. She is thankful for
her friends, who have faithfully stuck by her, and adjusted
their lives to accommodate her wheelchair. When was the
last time you thanked the Lord for your abilities? When
was the last time you thanked Him for your friends?

We can learn important things from people who have
experienced suffering. For one thing, they know self-pity
is destructive; that people who feel sorry for themselves
cut themselves off from blessings all around them. Shelly's friends love her because of her optimism and her courageous spirit.

I know what it is to be in need, and I know what it is to have plenty. I have learned the secret of being content in any and every situation, whether well fed or hungry, whether living in plenty or in want. I can do everything through him who gives me strength. (Philippians 4:12-13, NIV)

Chapter 19

Mr. Right—And Proud of It

Duane:

Not only am I Mr. Right,
I'm Mr. Perfectionist.
My mom says I was born neat.
They all laugh and think it's funny
to compare me with my sisters.
The truth is,
I like knowing and doing what's right.
　I like following instructions,
　　being on time,
　　meeting deadlines,
　　wearing pressed shirts,
　　studying at a clean desk,
　　getting the best score on Math quizzes,
　　keeping my car washed,
　　working out,
　　eating right,
　and I really hate to fail or do a bad job.
I *hate* it.
　　I don't like to try new things until
　　I'm sure I'll succeed.

I don't thank the Lord for failure,
   only success.
Is that being hard on myself?

Thought for Today:

Do you think it's true that we can't change? That this minute we are the way we'll be forever? What a terrible thought! One wonderful part of belonging to the Lord Jesus is the freedom He gives us to grow and change. There is nothing wrong with liking things to be right, but the perfectionist can be an unhappy person in an imperfect world. Besides, you won't gain any more respect, or friends, for being an arrogant perfectionist than you will for being a nice, average person. The perfectionist tends to make those around him very uncomfortable because he or she is frustrated with the imperfect world. Things are never perfect *enough* for the perfectionist. People, events, circumstances, even inanimate objects can set the perfectionist off on a grumbling binge.

It's OK to like things done the way you think is right, and it's fine to be an achiever. These are good points, and I encourage you to enjoy yourself with this in mind. But any preference, taken to an extreme, becomes insufferable when it is enforced with judgments and complaints.

God tells us that He is the only perfect One. When we allow Him to perfect us, it's liberating, not confining or restraining.

If we live in the Spirit, let us also walk
in the Spirit. (Galatians 5:25, NIV)

Chapter 20

How Come?

Debbie:

How come
no matter how hard you work
to get an A,
you usually come out with a B?
How come
when you do extra credit,
get to class on time,
are never absent,
hand in all the assignments
on time
and do your homework—
how come you *still* don't get an A?
How come
when you've practiced the piano
every day
since your first lesson
at age three,
you don't place at the piano competition?
How come
when you wash your face

twice a day with Physohex
and never eat greasy food,
you still break out?
How come
when you starve yourself
to be thin,
people still call you chubby?
How come
when you're nice to everybody
and try to get everyone to like you
and you're a good dresser,
your hair is perfect,
you still don't get to be
homecoming queen?
How come
bad things happen
when you're trying to be so good?
How come
hard work doesn't always
pay off,
and how come
when you've been sweet and obedient
and the ideal kid,
they're still getting a divorce?

Thought for Today:

The painful things in life that happen aren't all your fault. It's a helpless feeling to be unable to stop bad things from happening. Even when you do everything right, things can still go wrong. Parents' divorces bring pain to everyone involved, including the children. It's like watching a tornado heading toward your house and there's nothing you can do. The tornado still hits.

Bad things *do* happen to good people and that's one reason why we so desperately need a Savior. We know that the Lord does save us from a lot of harm and danger, but not entirely. He allows us to experience enough pain and hurt to become strong and beautiful Christians.

The good news is that God equips us to fight the battle, and He does deliver us from the effects of wrong, evil, bad, and Satan's attacks.

Pray that evil won't snag you in its teeth and damage your mind and emotions. Your feelings are important to God. When things don't go right, don't despair. If you're not homecoming king or queen, remember you're wearing a crown and a robe in God's eyes. You're permanent royalty where He's concerned.

And if you don't make the football team and you get shin splints before the track meet, you are still one of God's top athletes pressing toward the mark of the high calling in Christ Jesus (Philippians 3:14).

And those who know Thy name will put their trust in Thee; for Thou, O Lord, hast not forsaken those who seek Thee. (Psalm 9:10)

Part Three

ALMOST MAKING IT

Chapter 21

Morning Before School

Barbara:

Good morning, Jesus.
Time for me to get up
and get ready for school.
On second thought,
maybe I'll be sick instead.
I didn't finish my homework—
I still have three history chapters to read.
I can't go.
I think I'm coming down with something.
Lord, how am I supposed to love mornings
when I have Mr. Zork first hour?
But then if I stay home,
I'll miss music and English
and Felicia will kill me
if I don't return her biology notes.
Oh, Lord, so much to think about
and try to figure out:
>   Why didn't I do my homework?
>   Why is French so hard for me?
>   Does Mark like me or not?

Why can't I lose weight
or get along with my mother?
Oh, Lord, I love you,
but I'm sure I'm sick. Maybe I'll go back to sleep
and just miss first hour.

Thought for Today:

Have you ever felt like Barbara? She forgot that the problems will still be there when she wakes up, and she'll feel even worse about herself. Facing negative situations, failure and pressure is not easy. But putting it off, avoiding it and running away only makes your inner struggle more difficult.

When you feel like Barbara does, and you worry that you're not smart enough or good enough, thin enough, popular enough, or whatever, ask yourself: Does God agree with me?

According to His Word, what does He say about your potential? Does He indicate anywhere that you're doomed to fail French, or to repeat algebra, or never be liked by anyone of the opposite sex?

When you examine the truth in God's Word, you'll get a different outlook on life: you can do *all* things through Christ who strengthens you (Philippians. 4:13). When the apostle Paul said those words, he was talking about doing things well or doing them poorly; winning or losing. He 22uld enjoy abundance as well as suffer need because he had the strength of the Lord.

We need strength from God when we feel anxious or worried. To curl up in despair with the covers over your head is to lose out on the power of God. In Christ, you have perfect love to cast out fear and you have the Holy Spirit to help and teach you.

*F*or He delivered us from the domain of darkness and transferred us to the kingdom of His beloved Son. (Colossians 1:13)

Chapter 22

Frustration in English Class

Christy:

I want to be
a great writer someday.
But why do I have to know
all this stuff about
pronouns, verbs,
articles and prepositions?
Did Geronimo know that
buffalo was a noun
before he hunted it?
Did Attila the Hun
know to let his
participles dangle
or his tenses shift?
Did Joan of Arc
care if she used faulty parallelism?
What's wrong with my sentence,
"The caucasian male proved a harbinger of glad tidings"?
Mr. Jones wrote on my paper:
He "brought good news" will suffice.
If I spent vacation at my

grandmother's house, why can't I say,
"The respite from study was devoted
to a sojourn at the ancestral mansion"?
Mr. Jones says its journalese.
He says I use too many euphemisms.
(I had to look up *euphemism*.)
What about e.e. cummings
who didn't capitalize anything?
The apostle Paul
said things like,
"Moreover, brethren, I declare
unto you the gospel which I preached unto you,
which also ye have received, and wherein ye stand."*
(If he had Mr. Jones for English comp.,
his scrolls
would have been red-pencilled for sure.)
I feel my creative genius
is being stifled;
I'm suppressed and forced into a mold
by modifiers, transitional phrases,
and fear of neologisms.
(I had to look up *neologisms*.)
When, oh, when
do I get to be I?

Thought for Today:

Some things just aren't fun to learn. But if you learn them anyhow and don't try to avoid them, small miracles can happen. Every writer, linguist, and communicator has to learn grammar.

When in your life will you be dissecting frogs again? And when will you ever use the information you researched on the modern yellow-bellied sapsucker or the demise of Egyptian Sakhmet worship in 1400 BC? How

---

*1 Corinthians 15:1

Chapter 23

God Loves the Indians

Mark:

Bob was sitting next to me one day in English class, half asleep, when Mr. Jones stood up in front of the class and started to read this poem:

> The hands of God are like open plains
> and we travel them in our prayers . . .

He stopped reading and looked at us, just sitting there, and told us to write down what the metaphor he just read meant to us personally.

Bob started scribbling and drew a picture in his notebook of this guy riding a big dog—at least, that's what I thought it was until he told me it was supposed to be a buffalo. I wrote how I think God waits for our prayers with open hands because He wants to answer us. By the time I was done, Bob was practically snoring and Mr. Jones started to read again:

> And when we go the route of selfish gains,
> the fingers of God are locked into our cares . . .

He stopped again, and told us again to write what these

words meant to us. I looked at Bob—his head was nodding. Finally, he woke up enough to write, "God loves the Indians." I wrote how we need to stay close to the Lord and not get out of His reach.

> So God will bless us if we stay
> in His keeping every day,
> not traveling far from the fold
> where winter's fingers keep us cold.

Bob didn't hear that part—he was out. Mr. Jones finally noticed and told somebody to wake him up. I smiled to myself, and wrote something about how I wanted to stay close to God.

Mostly, though, I thought about how He loves the Indians.

Thought for Today:

God speaks to individuals in many different ways. What you get out of a song or a poem, for example, may be entirely different than what someone else gets out of it.

We limit ourselves with narrow thinking. When we try to conform our thoughts to what everyone else is thinking, we stifle the creativity and imagination God put inside of us, to make us unique. Don't be afraid to explore new ideas. Don't be afraid to move to the edge of the mold everyone else is in. God's arms can reach you—and His big hands will catch you—even there.

> *F*inally, brothers, whatever is true,
> whatever is noble, whatever is right,
> whatever is pure, whatever is lovely,
> whatever is admirable—if anything is
> excellent or praiseworthy, think about
> such things. . . ." (Philippians 4:8)

102

Do not conform any longer to the pattern of this world, but be transformed [by the renewing of your mind]. Then you will be able to test and approve what God's will is—His good, pleasing and perfect will. (Romans 12:2, NIV)

Chapter 24

The Perils of Facing the School Counselor

The following are based on samples of student letters received by high school guidance counselor Sue Kauth*. Every September, she says her office is overrun with students wanting to change their class schedules. The reasons they give do not always reflect the real reason for the requested change. Here are some adapted examples of letters Ms. Kauth might receive on a typical morning the first week of fall semester.

———

Dear School Counselor:

I am writing this letter to you because for some reason I got put in Mr. Wardle's western civilization class and I need to be in Mr. Snurdley's class. My sister had Mr. Snurdley for western civilization and learned quite a lot. I think he is the only teacher who can really make me understand our culture. . . .

Eager to Learn

*Marie Chapian *First Thursday,* Volume 1, Issue 5, September 1988. Blue Book Publishers, San Diego, Calif.

Dear Eager:

I can imagine why you think Mr. Snurdley is the only teacher who can make you understand our culture. Your sister bootlegged several of the exams last year. I also happen to know of a certain boy in Mr. Snurdley's class whom you want to study even more than our culture.
(P.S. You're the first teenager I've met who really wants to understand western civilization.)

———

Dear School Counselor:

Please take me out of Mr. Findle's advanced English class and put me in the lowest level English class there is. I want to really like and grasp the fundamentals of punctuation and all that stuff.

Sincere Sophomore

Dear Sincere:

You are perfectly capable of taking college preparatory English with Mr. Findle. Preparing for your future is even more important than the car I happen to know your folks have promised you if you make straight A's. With a little effort, you can have both!

———

Dear School Counselor:

I just can't have Mr. Gork again this year. Please change my advanced electronics class to Mr. Mottle's. I seemed to have a bad communication problem with Mr. Gork.

Concerned Communicator

Dear Concerned:

He communicated you right down to the Dean's office the last time you played your Walkman in class. I'd be happy to help but you need this class. Change *your* attitude and you'll be amazed to discover his probably will, too.

Thought for Today:

You must admit stretching the truth can be quite creative. But the difference between the Christians and non-Christians is that the Christians dare to tell the truth. *And* be creative about it. Suppose these studies have told the truth. Do you think they would have gotten better results? As a Christian you can risk everything and tell the truth because the truth lasts forever and even a good lie lasts only a short time. Might as well face the truth—God loves you and when you change your attitudes you'll find you usually get the results you want without "stretching the truth."

W hoever is careful about what he says protects his life. But anyone who speaks without thinking will be ruined. Good people hate what is false. But wicked people do shameful and disgraceful things. (Proverbs 13:3, 5, TEB)

Chapter 25

The Little Things

Felicia:

I've tried concentrating
on the little things
in life,
like eating my popcorn
more slowly,
not chewing my fingernails—
things like that.
I even started to think about
being neat;
I *typed* my report on the Federalist Papers.
Then along comes cell division in biology
and using the microscope
and I just freaked.
I mean, all that stuff going on
we don't know about.
And it's so orderly,
so perfect.
The more I'm learning
about the little things,
the more I'm learning about God.

109

If He thought enough
of the one-celled amoeba
and gave it a life,
continually changing,
engulfing its food
and multiplying by fission,
He can provide for me.

Kerry:

I've discovered
God is the Lord of protozoa,
cocci, bacilli and spirilla,
and He is the Lord of *my* life.
The God of oxygen and nitrogen
is the very Lord who walked in Galilee.
The Lord of refracted air waves,
of atoms and molecules,
of carbon dioxide,
plankton and the food chain
is the same God who answers my prayers.
The Lord of electromagnetic radiation,
gamma rays, X-rays,
ultra violet, radar, shortwave,
infrared, visible light and sound,
Lord of manometers, Kelvin and the sun
is the God who gave me a Savior
and who says He *loves* me.
When I learn about the wonders
of God's world, I discover I'm the one
who is the littlest of all.

Thought for Today:

The more you learn of creation, the more you learn
about God's character, and the more your faith will soar!

The apostle Paul said that ever since the creation of the world, the invisible attributes of God and His eternal power and divine nature have been clearly seen and understood through His creation, so that no one can doubt the existence of God (Romans 1:20).

Knowledge cannot destroy faith. The way you handle that knowledge, however, will either tear down or build up faith. King David was a poet and student all his life; he marveled and applauded the works of God. He loved to give thanks to God and testify to others of how God continued to work in his life and in the lives of the Israelites. He was awed by the wonders of creation:

When I consider Thy heavens, the works of Thy fingers, the moon and the stars, which Thou hast ordained; what is man, that Thou dost take thought of him? (Psalm 8:3, 4).

Your world is there for you, just waiting to be discovered!

O Lord, our Lord, how majestic is Thy name in all the earth! (Psalm 8:9)

Chapter 26

I Want My Life to Count for Something

A Prayer

I want my life to count
for something.
I want to stand and shout
the one thing
I believe:
  that I can do
  what the world says I cannot.
I can weave the plot
my life will follow,
sing with the voice of the wind
avoid the shallow,
reap the rewards of discipline.
I want
  to fly where stars make their beds,
  soar far above the common heads.
I want to ride the hem
of the robe of God
and go where no one
can condemn—
there I'll be

safe
and happy.
For when I face Him
I will lift my chin
and tell Him that all I did
I did for Him.

Thought for Today:

The Scriptures tell us that we can do all things through Christ who strengthens us. That's amazing when you think how we're limited by thinking only of ourselves and our immediate problems. What we sometimes forget is that all things change—your likes, dislikes, desires and dreams.

The only thing that won't change is the truth that your loving God strengthens you every day. Dream beautiful. Dream big. Make your life count for something. Do it for the Lord Jesus whose love reaches far beyond your limitations.

Remember this: the person who plants a little will have a small harvest. But the person who plants a lot will have a big harvest. (2 Corinthians 9:6, TEB)

Chapter 27

Who Understands Me?

Bob:

Half the time nobody understands me.
   Teachers think I'm someone I'm not,
my friends don't really know me,
   and my parents are like strangers.
How am I supposed to be myself
   when the whole world has me mixed up
with someone else?
   One day I'm going to meet this guy
that people have me confused with.
   And I'm going to say,
"So *you're* the class clown
in biology who's never serious."
I'll say,
"*You're* the guy who only thinks
about sports and girls."
And "What's it like to be
   a teenager who never talks to his poor parents?"
At night when I'm alone I read my Bible, and
   it tells me of One who understands—
One who sees me for who I really am.

I pray and ask Him to help me dare
to be the person *He* knows
    as me.

Thought for Today:

If you were to ask eight different people to describe you, you might get eight different responses. Sometimes it's safer to be who people think you are than to be yourself. If people laugh at your jokes and you like being funny, people might see only that side of you. If you're a good student and like to study and get good grades, you may be known as the Class Brain. But you are more than one or two descriptions. Your own personality is multifaceted, like a diamond, and you have to allow yourself to be and feel all that is within you. Be yourself to the fullest, and don't worry whether or not everybody can see and appreciate all of you.

All my ways are before Thee. (Psalm 119:168)

Chapter 28

Being Judged Is No Fun

Stephen:

No, you still don't understand.
It's not my bad points I worry that
    people will recognize.
It's the good ones that they seem
    to have a problem with.
I think the world must wait,
watching me through a microscope.
    The minute I begin my day,
out pop the judges.
"Here he comes, on time as usual."
    When I hand in a paper
that I've worked on half the night
    about a subject I actually *like*,
I can almost hear the little elves
    behind the teacher's desk
smirking,
    "Something must be wrong.
    This paper's too *good*!"
"Did he copy that?"
    What I'm saying is,

how come nobody ever says
   what I need them to say?

Thought for Today:

You want to feel that you're cared about no matter how good or bad you seem to be. Nobody wants to be thought of only in terms of their disagreeable points. But disagreeable or not, you are precious and uniquely you. Jesus treasures you.

The truth is, though, a lot of people *won't* treasure you for all your good points. And it's OK. Really it is. It won't hurt you one bit to be misunderstood—as long as you realize how much the Lord loves you. That is why it is absolutely vital to be reading the Word, praying and staying close to Him. He will constantly remind you of how valuable you are. People might not do that.

Keep yourself in the love of God, waiting anxiously for the mercy of our Lord Jesus Christ to eternal life. (Jude 21)

I have called you by name, you are mine! (Isaiah 43:1)

Chapter 29

Instant in Season

Jeff:

What do you say when people ask you
about being a Christian?
If a stranger saw you on the street
and asked you, "Hey, are you a Christian?"
would you reply, "Yes, I'm *saved*"?
How would you answer if the stranger said to you,
"How did you do that—
get saved?
What does that mean?"
Could you answer?
One girl I know couldn't remember.
"I got saved when I was real little," she said.
A stranger asked, "How?"
"I just asked Jesus into my heart," she said.
That was all she knew.
The stranger went away confused.
Oh, I think it's important
to be able to talk about the moment
our lives were reunited with God's Spirit,
to tell what happened

and keeps on happening—
what power lives within us,
surging, vibrantly pressing us forward, urging us on,
pushing supernatural strength
and wisdom into our hearts and minds,
creating, of mere flesh and bones,
something timeless, eternal,
exquisite, full of glory.
Because the Son of God gave His life on the cross
so His Spirit could lift us
beyond yourself to God.
Yes,
we ought to have an answer.
A stranger needs to know.

Thought for Today:

If you have a driver's license, do you remember the day you took the test? How did you feel when the examiner got into the car with you and told you to start the engine? Can you tell about how you parallel parked that day or when you had to make a sudden stop? And how about your score? Can you talk about what you got right and wrong? Chances are you can remember the experience well.

If you have a new car, can you tell about shopping for it, going to the car lot, choosing the vehicle, settling on the price, and finally holding the keys in your hand? Could you tell someone how it felt to drive your very own car for the first time?

Where does giving your life to Jesus fit in with these life experiences?

First Peter 3:15 says, "Always be ready to give a logical defense to any one who asks you to account for the hope that is in you" (Amp.). An example of a person who was always ready to give a testimony of his experience with God is David. Read his psalms and you will see how often David talks about what the Lord has done for him and how much He continued to do. You can be like David.

And this is that testimony—that evidence: God gave us eternal life, and this life is in His Son. He who possesses the Son has that life; he who does not possess the Son of God does not have that life. . . . These things have I written unto you that believe on the name of the Son of God; that you may know that you have eternal life, and that you may believe on the name of the Son of God. (1 John 5:11–13, Amp.)

Chapter 30

The Choice*

There once were three friends—
    an artist, a tailor, and a teacher—
        who went on a journey together.
They traveled for a long time,
    through the valley,
    up a steep mountain
    and into the forest.
One night, as the other two slept,
    the artist, who was keeping watch,
        carved the form of a woman out of a tree.
The next morning his friends were filled
    with admiration.
The tailor said,
    "I will create clothing for her."
The teacher said,
    "I will teach her to think and speak and read."
And so, they set to work.
        Soon the wooden figure was transformed

---

*From a Russian folk tale, "The Woman of the Wood."

into a soft and charming beauty.
The three friends were pleased with themselves,
    but not for long.
"She belongs to me," insisted the artist.
    "I shaped her from the tree with my own hands.
        That makes her mine!"
"She's mine!" the tailor protested angrily.
"Without my eye for design and style,
        her form would be drab and lifeless."
"You're both wrong!" cried the indignant teacher.
    "She's mine—I've taught her who she is
        and how to express herself."
The friends could not agree, and so
        they decided to seek the counsel of a wise old man
            who lived in a quiet corner of the king's palace.
"Tell us whom the woman belongs to,"
coaxed the friends,
        "and we will honor your decision."
The old man listened to their arguments,
        stroked his mottled beard, and said:
"Yes, I can see why the artist claims this woman as his
own.
        After all, he carved her out of the wood. . . .
On the other hand, the tailor has given her an exquisite
        and refined beauty. . . . Why shouldn't he claim her?"
He paused, then added, "And what does life mean to any
of us
        without knowing who we are, or why?
The teacher's claim is just, as well."
    The three friends held their breath,
        each confident of his own success.
Then the wise man looked at the woman,
        who had not yet spoken
            but only sat, quietly listening.
This time he spoke firmly:
    "Do we not belong to God alone?
How can your gifts—or even your sacrifices—

pay the price of ownership?"
The three friends were silent. The old man spoke again.
"I say this woman belongs to none of you. She is free.
   If she wishes to choose one of you, she can.
   But no man can choose for her.
   Not even you, who have done so much for her."
Now the woman lifted her head.
   To the amazement of the three friends,
      she began to speak.
"I thank you, artist, tailor and teacher,
   for all that you have given
      to make me what I am.
I am grateful, yet sad,
   for though I am a person now,
      I am still wood to you."
Then she turned to the wise old man,
   whose wrinkled cheeks were nearly hidden
      by his spindly white hair and ragged beard.
"You have done the most for me," she said.
   "You have given me freedom to choose.
      So I choose you."

Thought for Today

You can choose. You can allow yourself to be captivated, to be molded by those around you who want to make you conform to their imperfect image. Or you can be transformed into a Christlike young person, with His image stamped upon your heart.

It is not easy to make this choice. At times it is easier to run with the crowd, to get pulled into the flow. There will be people who may sound convincing—it may be the teacher who wants you to become "enlightened" from the "myths and legends" they think are in the Bible. Maybe it will be a "friend" who wants to get you to "loosen up," to let down your guard and compromise your principles.

Maybe it will even be one of your parents, who does not understand your commitment to Jesus Christ and puts down your faith. These kinds of people want to control some part of you—your behavior, your beliefs ... the things that make you uniquely you. They want to make you like them.

Jesus is the only One we should try to be like. He never forces people to love Him—He waits for them to become aware of His love for them, so they will come freely. The wise old man in the story knew that this is the only kind of love that matters. Jesus loves you and wants you to love Him back.

Nobody can "own" anybody else. We have choices about our lives that are ours alone. Choose Jesus today.

It is for freedom that Christ has set us free. Stand firm, then, and do not let yourselves be burdened again by a yoke of slavery. (Galatians 5:1, NIV)

But if serving the Lord seems undesirable to you, then choose for yourselves this day whom you will serve. . . . As for me and my house, we will serve the Lord. (Joshua 24:15)

Part Four

EMOTIONS COUNT

Chapter 31

Talk About Moms

Karen:

Somebody told me once
    that when we get to heaven,
God will judge us
    by how good we've been.
That scares me.
    I don't think
    I'm as good as some people.
My mom, for instance—
    she's really good.
She does good things for so many people
    and is always kind and nice.
Sometimes I hate being nice.
    And there are some people
I just don't like.
There's this guy Marvin in my English class.
    He's always got his hand in the air
with the right answers.
    I can't stand him.
He thinks he knows everything.
    He sits there smirking

as if the rest of us
    never heard of Chaucer or e. e. cummings.
My mother, though, would probably
    be nice to Marvin.
She would listen to what he had to say
    (he only talks about himself)
and offer him cookies
    and invite him to dinner.
I don't think I will ever be like my mother.
    Will I get to heaven?

Dawn:

My mother works two jobs.
    When I get up in the morning,
she's already gone.
    When I get home from school,
she calls to say hi
    and I make my own dinner.
I try to stay awake long enough
    to see her when she gets home at night,
but sometimes it's too late.
Her only day off is Sunday
    and then she's too tired
to do anything with me.
    I keep praying she'll
get a job that pays enough
    so she could be home at night
because we never go to church.
    Lately we don't even pray together.
I feel guilty she has to work so hard.

Steven:

I live with my dad in the winter

and my mom in the summer.
They divide me up
    that way.
Sometimes, I wish I could stay
    with my dad in the summer
because I miss my friends.
    But I can't;
I think he's glad to see me go
    sometimes.
But my mom is always sad
    when it's time for school again
and I have to go back to Dad's.
    She worries about me and cries.
But she doesn't ask questions
    about my stepmom anymore.
Dad goes to church; mom doesn't.
    Sometimes it's confusing,
But I pray for them,
    and then I pray for me.

James:

I get along with my mother—
    usually.
But she has a bad temper,
    and screams a lot.
My two sisters get the worst of it,
    and it's hard when she treats me
    better.
She makes them cook and clean,
    but not me.
She does my laundry,
    makes my lunches,
and makes them do those things
    themselves.
Ever since my dad walked out

five years ago when I was ten,
I'm supposed to be the man of the house.
How can a ten-year-old
be a man?
My sisters call me a male chauvinist pig.
Maybe I am,
but I really don't want to be.
I want to be what God says I should be,
but Mom doesn't always let me.
I feel as if I've missed out on a childhood.
As if I've never been young.

Thought for Today:

Karen worries about getting into heaven because she's not as "good" as her mom. Do you think your mom is better than you? You shouldn't; nobody is better than anybody else.

God doesn't judge us by how we measure up to other people, but by our love for Him. The Bible says all have sinned and are fallen short of the glory that God enjoys and extends to us (Romans 3:23). Only His grace through Jesus Christ puts us in right standing with Him and gets us into heaven. Your Lord takes your sins on himself, and presents you faultless to the Father.

Dawn's mom works so hard there's not even time for church; their family life is suffering as well. When a family's spiritual life is neglected, that family's only Source of real help is cut off. A home that is truly Christ-centered may have problems, and there may be arguments from time to time, but the Lord is always there to help resolve those conflicts. Forgiveness is an essential part of living in a Christian family—for both parents and teenagers.

James and Steven have been profoundly influenced—consciously or otherwise—by their mothers' mistaken ideas concerning the roles of men and women. James is being taught that caring for a family's daily needs is "woman's work." Unfortunately, this confuses and distorts his understanding of women and of his own masculinity. Young people need positive role models to help them mature in these areas.

It is important to pray for your mom, no matter how wonderful or terrible you think she is. She is as valuable to God as you are, and she deserves your respect just because she is your mom. The Bible says when you pray for your parents it will be well with you, and you'll live a long and good life (Ephesians 6:1–3).

Write a poem about your mom.

*B*eloved, if God loves us so very much, we also ought to love one another. (1 John 4:11)

Chapter 32

Talk About Dads

Jeff:

I went to a psychiatrist once.
    My parents were in therapy
and they dragged me along
    so he could ask me
to name the things in life
    I'm afraid of.
I thought, *You've got to be kidding!*
    What makes you think I'd tell you?
So I said,
    "There's nothing I'm afraid of."
But I've had these nightmares
    ever since I was three
of being chased by a big guy
    with knives.
I can't stand being in the car
    with my dad
when he's been drinking.
I never know when we'll move again
    and I'll have to make all new friends
again.

And I break out in a cold sweat
    at the smallest thought
that one day soon
    —I might turn out like my dad.

Jeremy:

When I was a kid,
    my dad carried me on his shoulders
and played "horsie."
    When I grew older, he taught me
how to throw a football
    and hit a baseball.
He took me fishing
    and to the library.
He taught me how to make

his special powerhouse pancakes,
and when I burned them
    he ate them anyway.
He played "Go to the Dump" and "War"
    with me,
and Monopoly and checkers and pick-up-sticks
    as though he really loved it.
He liked my friends,
    and took us all to the beach,
the car cram-packed
    with food and blankets, balls and boys.
People like my dad
    because he says
what he means
    and he thinks
all people are important.
    But when he says the words "my son,"
it seems he grows a little taller.
When he prays for me,
    I always know he has God's ear.
He taught me how to drive last year,
    and when I failed my drivers' test,
he was there
    to pat me on the shoulder.
He told me he failed
    his first test, too.
I never had a cowboy hero,
    a space hero or a movie hero,
because my dad will always be
    my real life hero.

Barbara:

Every day Dad
    goes to work,
        comes home,

sits in his chair,
eats dinner,
watches TV,
goes to bed,
and gets up for work
—That's his life. All of it.
People ask me if we're close.
I say, "Sure."
—But then I think about it.
We don't talk much,
at least not about important things.
We don't ever do anything alone
or go someplace just the two of us
without the rest of the family.
He doesn't ask me if I'm happy
and when I say, "I love you, Daddy,"
—he says, "Me, too."
He's not mean or anything.
He does lots of nice things.
He drives us places
and buys ice cream.
I'm busy with my friends and school, and
I babysit a lot,
but still
it's a shaky feeling to realize
my dad's been there my whole life
and I still don't know him.

Tom:

I can feel my dad's thin arms
around me and I can hear his
voice. He likes to talk about music
and philosophize.
"Remember Son," he said,
When the strings of a violin are loose,

140

they groan,
and when they're too tight,
they screech,
but balanced and tuned,
the violin makes beautiful music.
"There's honor in hard work," he said.
"Many a rich man is a miserable man," he said.
I used to hate his coughing
and the smell of sickness,
but now I'm so afraid I'll forget
his sounds and his stories.
A tight, gray fog
envelops me when I remember
there was nobody with him
when he died in his room
last September.
I'd give anything at all
if I could have him back again.

Thought for Today:

Your dad needs your prayers, no matter what your situation. If you are from a one-parent home, pray twice as much for that one parent.

Jeff, Jeremy, Barbara and Tom each have unique situations at home. Yours is unique too. It's a mistake to think that there is *one* certain way a family should be.

Have you ever wished you had a *normal* family? What is a normal family? Your dad may be different than other dads, and he might not treat you the way you want to be treated. But the fact is, you cannot change him. He might never be what you wish he could be.

Sometimes dads are critical, and seem to be looking for flaws in their kids. You can argue, fight, feel bad, cry, punch the wall, or run away; but unless your parents get help understanding themselves, they may not change the way they act. Some dads don't praise or reward their children. Some neglect discipline, and others discipline too harshly. The "perfect" dad is rare, but then again, that "perfect" anybody is rare. Accept your dad for who he is. Pray for him.

Beloved, let us love one another, for love is from God. (1 John 4:7)

Chapter 33

Wings

Sheri:

My mom says
there are two lasting things
she wants me to have:
one is roots;
the other, wings.
She says when I fly, she flies.
Well, Mom, I've gotten a new insight
on the word "grounded."
I'm sorry you won't be
up in the clouds today.

———

That's the problem with failure:
you always drag other people down with you
when you blow it.

———

I dreamed I'd be a doctor,
or a foreign diplomat.
Now I don't think I'll even get into college.

You can't be a pilot with bad eyes.
And you can't be a high school sophomore with a baby.
But how do I tell her?
Mom always made me believe
I was her special blessing.
How do I tell my friends,
or my little brother?
Mom was so proud to give me roots.
I guess I just couldn't manage
the wings.

Thought for Today:

Outside of marriage, having sex is like playing with a loaded gun—sooner or later, somebody is going to get hurt. Sex is not an indication of maturity or proof of love. In fact, it usually proves just the opposite, because pressuring someone into something that he knows is wrong demonstrates a selfish lack of concern for the other person.

Teenage pregnancy is both emotionally traumatic and dangerous. When it is not the aftermath of rape, such a pregnancy is usually the outcome of a few fleeting passionate moments.

Our media-oriented society bombards us with sensual messages. For "fun and profit" sex is smeared on screens, blown up on billboards, and used as a drawing card in every book and magazine rack in the country. Nudity, profanity, and sexual promiscuity are passed off as entertainment.

In the midst of all this, Christians are expected to remain pure, resisting temptation.

Fear of pregnancy won't ensure virginity. This is often the reason young people give for not having sex, but it is not a good reason. Conviction, not fear, should be the motivating force behind a person's behavior. The teenager who maintains his (or her) sexual purity is psychologically better prepared for adulthood, because self-control reflects integrity and strong values. This makes him or her a responsible person. If you make choices that violate your beliefs of what is right and wrong, you retard your own growth and dignity.

Deeply rooted, Christ-centered values are your only sure defense. When your values are rooted in God's Word, you have a source of help and information to instruct you as you grow to maturity, and to help you understand your own sexuality.

Of the hundreds of teenagers I've talked to, including the ones who speak in this book, not one of them has told me they regretted abstaining from sex and waiting until marriage, even though at times it was very difficult. One seventeen-year-old young man told me, "The sex drive doesn't go away, especially when I'm with my girlfriend . . . but I've decided to control the drive instead of it controlling me."

We live in a confused whirl of sexual madness that is destroying and killing people, an era of disease and psychological angst. You cannot judge what is right and wrong by what "everybody else" is doing, because our society's value system is breaking down rapidly. Ernest Hemingway said that moral is what you feel good after and immoral is what you feel bad after.

That's not what God says. He tells us to guard our passions, to put a watch on our appetites and fix our minds on what is good and pure and wholesome. Your body is a temple, where the Spirit of God lives. Your body should be as clean as your heart, which was washed pure by the blood of Jesus. Your conscience is your friend; listen to it.

Be responsible for your actions. It's unfair for a girl to tease and provoke a boy and it is unfair for a boy to pressure a girl to "prove" her love. You are the only one responsible for you.

Do you not know that your body is the temple . . . of the Holy Spirit Who lives within you, Whom you have received [as a Gift] from God? You are not your own, you were bought for a price—purchased with a preciousness and paid for, made His own. So then, honor God and bring glory to Him in your body. (1 Corinthians 6:19, 20, Amp.)

I have strength for all things in Christ Who empowers me—I am ready for anything and equal to anything through Him who infuses inner strength into me. (Philippians 4:13, Amp.)

Chapter 34

Anger

Jeff:

Everything makes me angry.
I hate to get up
when I want to sleep in.
I go crazy
when I lose something.
I can't stand it
when my mother nags.
I get angry
when my brother wants to borrow something.
I don't like
to be told what to do,
and I can't stand
dumb people who get in my way.

———

If God wanted me to be peaceful,
He shouldn't have created me
the way He did
and put me in the family He did,
and made me so helpless

when my dad gets mad.
If God didn't want me angry,
He would have given me a dad
who didn't drink and beat us up,
who didn't make me wish he'd die.
He would have given me the courage
to help my mother
before Dad broke her nose.
At school I punched a kid,
a skinny kid
with big scared eyes,
and I heard a voice say,
like a dagger of ice,
"He's just like his father."

Thought for Today:

Misplaced anger is being angry at one thing but directing it at someone or something else. Jeff is angry at his father's abusive behavior and his own helplessness to stop the violence. But whom does he take it out on? A defenseless kid.

If you are being abused, or are in some other life-threatening situation, *you must get help!* It is not always possible to take care of yourself. Sometimes you need to turn to others who will protect you. This is not always easy, because kids who are abused are usually made to feel guilty, so they won't go for help.

Remember, adults are responsible for their own actions, and must be held accountable for what they do. If you are being abused or know of someone who is being abused, get help. In some cases, a move to a safer, healthier place is necessary.

Jeff does not have to be just like his dad, and your genes are not automatically programmed to make you behave like someone you can't admire.

You can choose to feel anger, but you were not born angry. Every day is a new day, and every day your loving heavenly Father empowers you with strength to meet the challenges of that day. You can live in confidence and happiness in spite of the storms all around you.

God himself has said, "I will not in any way fail you nor give you up nor leave you without support. [I will] not, [I will] not, [I will] not in any degree leave you helpless, nor forsake nor let [you] down, [relax my hold on you].—Assuredly not!" (Hebrews 13:5, Amp.).

Anger is an important emotion. It tells you something vitally important about your life that you must not ignore. It doesn't go away by itself.

> The Lord is my Helper, I will not be seized with alarm—I will not fear or dread or be terrified. What can man do to me? (Hebrews 13:6, Amp.)

Chapter 35

Bad Habits

James:

Jesus, you are Lord of my life.
 I don't know why I do
some of the things I do.
 I lose my temper and swear
and fight with my sisters. . . .
 Lord, I have so many bad habits.
I'm like that dying seal I saw
 last week on the beach—
out of the water
 and gasping for breath
on dry, hot sand.
 I was born
to know you and serve you,
 but sometimes
I just don't act anything at all
 like a Christian.
Your Word says I have a new nature,
 and I want to live like it.
Your Word says to count myself
 dead to sin and alive to you.

I want to!
     Please channel my temperament to your glory,
     and help me to understand myself
in the light of your Word
     so bad habits won't defeat me
and separate me from you.

Thought for Today:

Constantly remind yourself that Christ lives in you, and the life you now live in your human body you live by faith in the faithfulness of the Son of God who loves you and gave himself for you (Galatians 2:20). You're not some weak thing the Devil can toss around like a toy.

Spiritual growth requires certain conditions. The first is a daily fellowship with the Lord, worshiping, praying, and just being with Him. Nothing chases Satan away faster. That's why he tries to make us believe we don't have enough time to pray or spend time with the Lord.

Teenagers have told me they need something to turn them on, to interest them when they try to read the Bible. It's hard to know where to start sometimes. Christian bookstores are well stocked with books and materials just for you. Christian youth magazines, devotional books, tapes, records and videos are waiting for you to discover.

It is useless to try to gain victory over sin and bad habits by our own efforts. Self-centeredness scrambles our thinking, and we become spiritually defeated. When you make the decision to live for God, you accomplish that by allowing Him to live *through* you.

When you stumble and fail, be assured that every Christian shares your problem. Even Charles Spurgeon, a great man of God, tells of his own experiences in the depths of depression over his sin. The apostle Paul also knew spiritual defeat because he was not perfect either. In desperation, he cried out to God, "O wretched man that

I am! Who shall deliver me from the body of this death?" (Romans 7:24). The body he speaks of is the self-centered part of man that wants to be in control, instead of giving that control over to God.

Ephesians 4:15 speaks of growing up into Him in all things. We are to grow in grace. Don't forget, though, your Christian life begins with your new birth in Christ and you need time to develop. You are still only a baby compared to the old sinful creature you've grown up as. Don't be too hard on yourself.

Instead of focusing on your weaknesses, ask God for forgiveness and go on. Pronounce yourself strong and free. Jesus has redeemed you from every bad habit and evil work. Sin does not control you.

Pray this prayer:

Father, in the name of Jesus and according to your Word, I claim Jesus as Lord of my life and my habits. From this day forward I refuse to have anything to do with the following bad habits: _____. Jesus died on the cross so I can withstand temptation. The Holy Spirit is my guide and my helper. I will not be lazy and neglect prayer. I will not be overcome with evil, but I will overcome evil with good. Amen.

Those who [live] according to the Spirit and [controlled by the desires] of the Spirit, set their minds on and seek those things which gratify the (Holy) Spirit. (Romans 8:5, Amp.)

Chapter 36

Why Can't Guys Have Long Hair?

Stephen:

Jesus had long hair, didn't He?
So did the apostles.
It really burns me up
how victimized we are by social customs.
Where in the Bible does it say
the hair of Christian males shall be
trimmed above the ear?
Where does it say
the heads of males shall not be shaved
unless they are in the army?
I can't understand
why my dad doesn't appreciate me
for the good person I try to be.
I don't take drugs,
I've never failed a class,
I get along with teachers,
I bus tables at
Pizza Hut after school.
And I never ask him for *anything.*
I buy my own clothes.

Why does it matter to him
that I like drawing better than baseball?
And that I play my guitar in my room
instead of watching the Olympics on TV?
All he talks about is my hair.
He told my stepmom
that for a guy I was good-looking,
but I sure made an ugly girl.
I don't think my dad knows
I have feelings.
I think he sees me as the enemy,
a person on the other side
who constantly
threatens him
with a loss of power.
Do I have to be overpowered
to be loved?
Do I have to be like *him*
before he'll be proud of me?

Thought for Today:

Maybe your dad will always seem critical and unlov-
ing, and maybe you will never get his approval. The ques-
tion is this: Are you capable of loving him anyhow? You
disapprove of him, too, you know.

When one or more of your parents disapproves of you,
it's pretty certain you disapprove of them, too. So there
are always these vibes of conflict in the air. Do you think
your dad is "shallow" for liking baseball more than art?

If you told me your parents approved of every move
you make, I'd think someone's lying. Surely *somebody's*
got to say to you once in a while, "You're not going out
in *that*, are you?" And an occasional dose of, "When are
you going to get that hair cut, Samson?" never hurt anyone. (Except Samson.)

Sometimes parents are like strangers from another planet, but you don't have to understand someone to love them. What do you do to encourage open discussions with your parents? Have you ever sat down with your dad to talk about your feelings? Have you listened to his feelings? How would you start an open discussion with your dad if you were Stephen?

> Let all bitterness and wrath and anger and clamor and slander be put away from you, along with all malice. And be kind to one another, tender-hearted, forgiving each other, just as God in Christ also has forgiven you. (Ephesians 4:31, 32)

Part Five

WALKING TALL

Chapter 37

When You Need Help

Becky:

Maybe I'm not a good Christian,
    but sometimes I get really tired
of the struggle and the hassle.
I just want to be happy
    and I want things to go right
without working for it.
    Other people have it easier than I
because they can just pray
    and everything is fine,
but not me.
    I'm different.

Calvin:

    Wrong.
You're not alone
    and not so different.
How come you think
    you're the only one

with struggles?
  Maybe prayer seems hard
because you don't know
  whom you're praying to.
When I talk
  to someone I know and like,
it's not the same as
  talking to a stranger.
When I know someone
  who really cares about me,
I want to talk to that person.
  I don't get tired of the struggle
because I love the One
  who never lets me struggle alone.

Lisa:

I had to learn
  to tell myself the truth—
that there will always be problems.
  So when they come
I say to myself,
  "Face them."
And I face them head-on,
  wearing the full armor
of God
  like in Ephesians 6.
And I thank Him
  for showing me
how to struggle
  and win.

Becky:

  I love Ephesians 6

and I really do love Jesus.
    Maybe you're right.
Maybe I need to know
    Him better.
Maybe I need to learn
    to enjoy winning
more than losing,
    and maybe I need you
to pray for me.
    Will you?

Calvin:

Father, in Jesus' name,
    you didn't create us
to be losers or weaklings.
    You didn't create us to live
as defeated teenagers.
    We are your children and your heritage.
We thank you that Becky
    is a child of the King.
Satan is the author of doubt and unbelief,
    but he has no power over Becky.

Lisa:

Father, you have written
in your Word that if we confess
    with our mouth that
Jesus is Lord
    and if we believe in our hearts
that you have raised Him
    from the dead,
we shall be saved.
    Becky made you Lord

163

of her life
	the day she became a Christian.
You give her the power
	to withstand the darts
of the evil one.
	And so we ask that you
draw her to a closer walk
	with you.
Let her love for you increase
	so she loves prayer
and loves her relationship
	with you
more than anything
	In Jesus' name.

Becky:

	Father, forgive me
of my sin of unbelief
	and doubt.
Forgive me
	for becoming lazy.
Thank you for Jesus, my Lord.
	Thank you for making me
a new creation.
	Old things and old feelings
pass away.
	Now all things become new.
Thank you for my friends who love you
	and care enough
to pray for me.

Thought for Today:

	Read this conversation one more time. Do you have
friends who pray for you? Do you pray for your friends?

*T*hen you will call the Lord, and the Lord will answer you. You will cry out to the Lord, and He will say, "Here I am." (Isaiah 58:9, TEB)

Chapter 38

Quiet Time

Jill:

In the quiet of the early morning, Lord,
I bring my thoughts to you.
    I turn off the radio
and I am quiet inside.
    I concentrate
on what you have spoken to me.
    Then I allow you
to walk into my soul,
    to lift me up,
to move where the real me lives.
    I feel myself awake,
not to the problems
    of the coming day,
but to you.
    I feel at one with you, Lord.
I feel your love and your concern,
    and it's what I love to feel.
I love the safety and peace
    that comes into me when I know
the day is in your hands.

I pray I can be an expression
of what you have given me.

Thought for Today:

The decisions you make and the goals you achieve are
directly linked to your prayer life. You are at a critical,
decision-making time of life. In the next five to ten years
you will make decisions about your education, career,
marriage, and ministry that will set the course for the rest
of your life.

Prayer is crucial. Through prayer and study of the
Word you learn His purposes. The most important decision of your life isn't where to go to college or what career
to choose but how to dedicate your life to working for the
purposes of God.

If we are called to fulfill the purposes of God, it begins
with caring for others; we can't possibly know how to do
this if we don't know how much God cares for *us.* And if
we are to have compassion for our world and for those
who need the Lord, we must know His heart.

I have been inspired by a vivacious and inspiring missionary who works with a little mission across the Mexi-
can border in Tijuana. She has to work an extra job to
support herself because the mission is poor. She gives the
donations that come for her support to the poor for food.
She told a group of students, "I invest four hours to travel
every day and eight hours to work because I want to serve
the Lord. I don't get much of a chance to sleep, but it is
important to serve God, more important than my own
comfort."

When asked where she gets all her energy, she said
simply, "In prayer." Prayer is her fuel. When you worship
God in prayer, your whole being becomes alive, renewed
and refreshed.

"Without prayer I wouldn't know how to handle the

tragedies of poverty and sickness I see every day," she told us. "I would just be overwhelmed emotionally, and I would be no use to God or anyone else."

What decisions are you facing today? Prayer is your fuel.

Give ear to my words, O Lord,
    consider my meditation.
Hearken unto the voice of my cry,
    my King, and my God:
for unto thee will I pray.
    My voice shalt thou hear
in the morning,
    O Lord; in the morning
will I direct my prayer
    unto thee and will look up.
(Psalm 5:1–3, KJV)

Chapter 39

Teen Prayer

The teenagers whose voices are heard in this book pray . . .

Father,
    in the name of Jesus we pray
        for young people like us
    who struggle with the same things
        we struggle with
    and who need you
        as much as we do.
Father,
    You know all about us;
        all about the problems
        we face growing up.
    Your thoughts for us
        are good and not evil.
We pray that those who read this book
        will keep their minds glued on you
        and will not allow themselves to become
            —agitated or disturbed
intimidated, fearful or unhappy.

We resist all these things
in the mighty name of Jesus.
Father,
We want to proclaim without shame
the love and joy and freedom
we have found in you.
Unite us as your teenage army,
and send us to our hungry world
where wars are fought
and people killed.
To every place that needs to hear
how much you love us.
Teach us, Lord,
that feeling small
is only temporary,
and that you are always with us
walking tall.

Scripture verses to look up:

Ephesians 6:10–19
Jeremiah 29:11–13
Isaiah 26:3
John 14:27
Psalm 1
Psalm 23:6
Matthew 28:19, 20